Your New Day Dawning

Each new day is a regeneration, a new day dawning for the earth. Jesus also gives us the chance each moment of each new day to be reborn and to start again as a new creation in Him, this is Your New Day Dawning.

Your New Day Dawning

Lady Kimberly Motes Doty

Lady Kimberly Motes Doty

ASIN: B0C5B6JFXR   Kindle
ISBN: 979-8394715778   Paperback
ASIN: B0C5B9YVR2
ISBN: 978-1-0882-5916-0
ISBN: 979-8394719936   Hardcover
ASIN: B0C5BMKDGC

Copyright © 2023 by Lady Kimberly Motes Doty and Lady Kimberly Industries, LLC

All Rights Reserved.

No part of this production may be reproduced, distributed, or transmitted in any form or by any means, including photocopying, recording, or electronic or mechanical methods without the prior written permission of publisher.

Dedication

To **God**, the ultimate source of inspiration and the creator of this magnificent world, I humbly dedicate this book, "Your New Day Dawning."

With deepest gratitude, I offer my thanks for your boundless grace and unwavering love, which have granted me the privilege of experiencing the splendor of the beach, the warmth of my cherished family and friends, and the countless opportunities that have propelled me back onto the path of my divine purpose. Your divine intervention has been my guiding light, allowing me to perceive angelic wings within an open clam shell, a resplendent heart nestled within an unassuming pen shell, your divine presence in a pure white feather, and the very essence of your soul in the radiant hues of a sunrise.

Just as each new day heralds the rebirth of our planet, Jesus Christ offers us the chance to be reborn in Him, embracing the opportunity to become a new creation. As 2 Corinthians 5:17 aptly reminds us, we need not remain confined to a life or a lifestyle that we find disheartening. Through Jesus, we can embark on a transformative journey, enabling us to shed our old selves and emerge as the genuine, best versions of ourselves.

May the pages of this book serve as a testament to the transformative power that resides within each one of us. May it inspire and encourage those who peruse its contents to embrace the dawn of a new day, to allow Jesus to mold them into a renewed creation, and to embark on a journey toward their truest, most authentic selves.

Lady Kimberly Motes Doty

In humble reverence and utmost gratitude, I offer this dedication to you, O Lord. May your presence illuminate the path of every reader, guiding them towards their own new day dawning.

As 2 Corinthians 5:17 tells us "If anyone is in Christ, he is a new creation; the old is gone, the new has come!"

"If anyone is in Christ, he is a new creation; the old has gone, the new has come!" 2 Corinthians 5:17

This is one of the examples in the Bible that is so important it has an explanation point at the end. I always love those because its a signal to me to pay extra attention to them.

This entire book is written around this inspirational verse, a verse of regeneration and renewal, of becoming a new creation.

Amen.

"If anyone is in Christ, he is a new creation; the old has gone, the new has come!"
2 Corinthians 5:17

Lady Kimberly Motes Doty

Acknowledgment

To My Family

To my family, for your amazing patience, love and understanding through all the updates and iterations of this book and all the others.

For sitting and most days, lying down with me, when I couldn't stand, and for endless hours of just being with me when that was all I was capable of doing.

For understanding some days I can walk for miles and other days I can barely move.

God knew I needed you most of all my family, my life, my inspirations, my dreams, my girls, my babies, my loves!

I love you always and forever.

Your Mom, Mamaw, & Mimi forever and ever!

Your New Day Dawning

To My Doctors

Dr. Asraf Hanna, MD

Pain Management, Florida Spine Institute

Dr Hanna, I want to express my deepest gratitude for the profound impact you have had on my life. Through your expertise and compassionate care, you not only restored my mobility but also gave me a renewed sense of hope. Dealing with an enduring and agonizing condition like Reflex Sympathetic Dystrophy (RSD) or Complex Regional Pain Syndrome (CRPS) can easily drown one in despair, pain, and depression.

Lady Kimberly Motes Doty

Your positive outlook on life and your genuine concern for my well-being prevented me from succumbing to the often-discussed fate of becoming a "suicide disease" statistic.

Unlike many doctors today who perceive patients as mere dollar signs, particularly in the realm of pain management, you demonstrated an unwavering commitment to seeing me as a person. Your approach went beyond the conventional medical paradigm, encompassing a thoughtful understanding of the multidimensional impact of my condition.

I express my utmost gratitude to you and your esteemed team for your unwavering patience, consistent provision of care, and empathetic understanding. Your unwavering support during those occasions when I struggle to perform even the simplest tasks due to immense pain, or when my toenails are literally burning off before your very eyes, or when I am filled with excitement over a movie role, or even when I find myself sobbing due to excruciating agony, and the days spent confined in a dark room battling a severe migraine, have not gone unnoticed.

Dr. Hanna, you have stood by my side throughout the majority of my arduous journey with RSD/CRPS, as well as during both my encounters with cancer, and the subsequent surgeries required for its treatment. Your comprehension of the peaks and valleys experienced by individuals with chronic pain conditions, along with the arduous recovery process from cancer, serves as the cornerstone of your consistently compassionate and exceptional care.

Your New Day Dawning

Being able to place my trust in you to manage my healthcare has been instrumental in enabling me to navigate through my health challenges and prioritize my well-being, rather than being consumed by concerns about my healthcare provider.

This sentiment holds immense significance for the countless individuals who struggle to locate a reliable physician, a healthcare professional who genuinely places their patients' health as the utmost priority.

You embody the qualities of a truly compassionate and virtuous individual, particularly during a period where the world is in dire need of healers like you, and healthcare providers who, like those in your employ, share your commitment to providing exceptional care. I consider myself truly fortunate to have the privilege of knowing you and benefiting from your expertise as my doctor.

Lady Kimberly Motes Doty

Dr Claudia Hays, MD

Obstetrician / Gynecologist, Anne Arundel Medical Center

Dr. Hays, I am infinitely grateful to you. Without your intervention and assumption of my medical care, it is impossible to fathom how long it would have taken for the cancer to be discovered. This is a question that only God can truly answer.

Your New Day Dawning

All I know is that my gratitude towards you and your team for their collaboration and support knows no bounds. In a time of great uncertainty, you welcomed me back as a patient, despite not having seen me in many years, and that act of compassion is something for which I cannot express enough appreciation.

Dr. Hays had served as my obstetrician/gynecologist (OB/Gyn) for the majority of the nearly two decades I resided in Maryland. Upon relocating to Florida, I initially sought the care of another OB/Gyn. However, when this doctor departed from the practice, I didn't bother establishing myself with a new provider, as my age rendered visits to the OB/Gyn infrequent. Once postmenopausal, it is generally recommended to undergo an appointment with an OB/Gyn only once every three years, unless specific health concerns arise. Consequently, the notion of cancer remained nowhere near my thoughts when I began experiencing troubling symptoms.

When experiencing postmenopausal bleeding, it becomes apparent that something is amiss. Despite attempts to secure an appointment with a different OB/Gyn in Florida, it proves exceedingly challenging to schedule an appointment with a new doctor once issues arise.

Lady Kimberly Motes Doty

The medical community exhibits reluctance to provide care when informed of ongoing problems, expressing a preference for understanding why the patient failed to seek medical attention for a few years, even though routine visits to an OB/Gyn are only recommended every three years assuming no complications. My own health had been satisfactory until it was not. Consequently, due to a two-year lapse since my last checkup, I encountered difficulties in accessing alternative medical care.

Over the course of approximately another year, I diligently made contact with no less than thirty, or perhaps even forty, medical practices in the state of Florida. My efforts encompassed reaching out to virtually every physician affiliated with my insurance network, as well as every practitioner within a thirty-mile radius as indicated by Google's search results, who purportedly accepted my insurance. Despite these extensive attempts, I encountered insurmountable difficulties in finding a healthcare provider willing to treat my condition, characterized by severe bleeding.

Eventually, feeling helpless and unsure of how to proceed, I decided to reach out to Dr. Hays, based in Maryland. Despite the passage of more than a decade since she last attended to my medical needs, she promptly accommodated my request for an appointment. Due to logistical constraints and the necessity for me to travel back to Maryland, several rescheduling instances were necessary. Nevertheless, I greatly appreciated the unwavering commitment displayed by Dr. Hays' office in working with me to ensure my access to her expertise.

Your New Day Dawning

The provision of patient care appears to have diminished significantly, with a lack of genuine concern for individuals' personal lives. Therefore, discovering a medical practice that exhibits such attentive behavior is undeniably fortuitous and, in my particular circumstances, life-saving.

During my initial consultation with Dr. Hays, she conducted a biopsy when considering the challenges I had been experiencing for well over a year. In a prompt manner, she contacted me to communicate that the biopsy results were disquieting and necessitated further comprehensive examinations. Consequently, I would have to return to Maryland and undergo these procedures within a hospital setting. Nonetheless, she managed to avoid instilling panic or excessive apprehension, reminding me that these anomalies could potentially signify significant health issues or, conversely, prove to be inconsequential.

A notable aspect of Dr. Hays' care was her dedication to spending time with my husband following the biopsies in the hospital, to provide a comprehensive explanation of her findings. She went beyond words by presenting him with vivid, full-color photographs depicting the suspected cancer, accompanied by detailed explanations for each image. This thoughtful approach shed light on the nature of the cancer, its potential implications, and the subsequent steps we would need to take as a family should the pathology confirm the diagnosis.

Lady Kimberly Motes Doty

In stark contrast, when my father faced cancer, none of the doctors extended this courtesy to my mother or any other member of our family, to the best of my knowledge. In the case of my mother's cancer, the doctor's efforts were limited to displaying, for a mere thirty seconds, the size of the mass in her chest on a computer screen, rendered in green and white. This method failed to convey the true significance of the tumor's size in relation to her body or offer any meaningful context beyond its nondescript appearance on the screen.

Two days later, shortly before the Thanksgiving holiday, Dr. Hays contacted me to deliver the definitive diagnosis of cancer. In addition, she provided a referral to an oncologist whom she personally trusted. With an intention to offer solace, she reassured me that the cancer had been detected early and assured me that everything would be alright.

Nonetheless, the mention of cancer had a profound impact, causing my world to crumble in an instant.

Dr. Hays, I am infinitely grateful to you. Without your intervention and assumption of my medical care, it is impossible to fathom how long it would have taken for the cancer to be discovered. This is a question that only God can truly answer. All I know is that my gratitude towards you and your team for their collaboration and support knows no bounds. In a time of great uncertainty, you welcomed me back as a patient, despite not having seen me in many years, and that act of compassion is something for which I cannot express enough appreciation.

Your New Day Dawning

There are instances where healthcare guidelines or recommendations may appear peculiar. In this particular case, the guidelines suggested that I, due to my age and absence of any underlying concerns, did not require medical attention more frequently than every three years. However, since I had not undergone an examination in two years, I encountered difficulties in seeking assistance when an issue arose.

It is disconcerting to observe that the individuals responsible for formulating these recommendations sometimes fail to adhere to or even exploit them to the detriment of patients. Regrettably, I found myself entangled in a predicament that nearly had fatal consequences.

Consequently, I have learned the importance of advocating for oneself in matters of healthcare. As an individual, you possess an intimate understanding of your own body and can discern what is right and what is not. It is crucial that you do not allow anyone to dismiss your concerns.

It becomes imperative to locate a healthcare provider who will listen attentively, as Dr. Hays did when I contacted her, and provide the necessary care when something is amiss. Patience may be required, especially for women, and particularly for older women like myself.

Lady Kimberly Motes Doty

If an issue arises that affects your well-being, persist until you locate a genuinely attentive individual who comprehends your requirements and is committed to caring for you. This process should ideally not be as arduous as it sometimes is; nevertheless, it remains preferable to the alternatives of enduring a debilitating condition or, worse yet, succumbing to it.

Do not mistake your efforts for assertiveness; you are simply extending the same love, compassion, and respect that you readily offer to others. It is perfectly acceptable to extend this same care to yourself.

Seek out healthcare providers such as Dr. Hanna, Dr. Hays, and those I acknowledge in my publications.

These doctors possess the rare and invaluable qualities bestowed upon them by God, namely, the knowledge and the genuine desire to assist people in a compassionate and respectful manner.

They prioritize providing compassionate and respectful treatment with the intention of facilitating genuine healing and improvement. After all, isn't genuine healing and improvement our ultimate goal in seeking their expertise?

Your New Day Dawning

Dr. Monica Jones, MD

Medical Director Gynecologic Oncology, Obstetrics / Gynecology, Anne Arundel Medical Center

Dr. Jones is the oncologist referred to me by Dr. Hays on the day she informed me of my cancer diagnosis.

In a state of tearful distress and mental confusion, I dialed the number provided by Dr. Hays. To my surprise, Dr. Jones personally answered the call, demonstrating that fate can manifest in unexpected ways.

I remember informing Dr. Jones about the news I had just received from Dr. Hays. Dr. Jones reassuring words of "don't worry, I've got you now" and "everything is going to be ok" are still in my dreams and sometimes nightmares to this day.

Lady Kimberly Motes Doty

A profound sense of tranquility and reassurance washed over me, affirming that her words were genuine and that all would be well. The circumstances leading to her answering that fateful phone call remain unknown to me, yet I am eternally grateful that she did so. In truth, I found solace in her presence and the knowledge that everything was indeed alright. It is remarkable how fate aligns individuals precisely where they are intended to be, and it was apparent that day when the Medical Director of the Gynecologic Oncology Department at what was then known as Anne Arundel Medical Center personally addressed my concerns.

Dr. Jones, despite undoubtedly being consumed by numerous obligations, graciously spared a few minutes of her precious time to engage in a conversation that would forever shape my existence. Her compassionate reassurances remain vivid in my memory, exemplifying her unwavering commitment to her patients.

I was promptly contacted by Dr Jones' patient care coordinator, Connie, demonstrating her dedication to our care. She provided consistent support and guidance throughout the entire process, ensuring that both my spouse and I were well-informed of the forthcoming stages. The exceptional level of patient care and coordination she exhibited proved invaluable to us.

For those who have experienced similar circumstances, the depth of understanding is profound. However, for those unfamiliar, allow me to elucidate. The sensation is akin to traversing an alternate reality, as if navigating one's life through a thick fog, where every movement occurs in sluggish motion.

Your New Day Dawning

The sense of realness becomes nebulous, with an eerie detachment from oneself, observing events unfold as though happening to another person amidst the cacophony of blaring music and flashing strobe lights.

Without individuals such as Connie, who possess an astute attention to detail, guiding us through such trying times, it becomes unimaginable to fathom how others endure these challenges.

The term "cancer" possesses a profound impact, causing one to pause and grapple with the unimaginable reality of its presence. In subsequent chapters, I delve into the notion of the "shadow of death," an apt description for the sensation of being engulfed by an ominous presence, encircling and enveloping one's very being. In navigating such trying circumstances, individuals like Connie are invaluable, as they possess the exceptional ability to guide us with their compassionate nature, attention to detail, and unwavering respect. Her approach, reminiscent of a virtuous woman guided by a higher power, resonates deeply within me, exemplifying a grace and dignity that will forever remain etched in my memory.

Within a brief span of approximately one week, Dr. Jones successfully eradicated the malignancy present in my body, effectively saving my life. Undoubtedly, my cancer removal procedure must have been a routine occurrence for Dr. Jones, an ordinary and commonplace event within her extensive experience in the field of gynecologic oncology surgeries. If memory serves correctly, my operation marked the approximate one-thousandth instance of such a procedure she had conducted. However, for me and my family, this surgical intervention forever altered the trajectory of our lives.

Lady Kimberly Motes Doty

Cancer possesses an innate ability to profoundly transform and redirect the lives of those it affects. It was not limited to just my life, as every single member of my family was deeply impacted by this disease.

Dr. Jones, I express my heartfelt gratitude for "having me" and providing me with an exceptional level of compassionate care. From our initial conversation to your collaboration with the anesthesiologist to mitigate the risk of a post-surgical RSD/CRPS flare-up, I am sincerely thankful for your profound understanding, unwavering compassion, and utmost respect in administering your care.

Your New Day Dawning

Dr Charles Hatcher, MD

Anesthesiologist, Anne Arundel Medical Center

Due to the presence of Reflex Sympathetic Dystrophy (RSD) or Complex Regional Pain Syndrome (CRPS) in my body, even the smallest trauma, such as a pin prick on my skin, has the potential to trigger a flare-up of RSD/CRPS, resulting in days or even months of severe burning pain.

Prior to my cancer surgery, I had the opportunity to explain this condition to Dr. Hatcher, the anesthesiologist, who went above and beyond to extensively research RSD and CRPS. His objective was to implement an appropriate Ketamine protocol during the surgery, aimed at minimizing the likelihood of a traumatic flare-up. This exceptional level of care exemplifies the compassionate approach embraced by the medical professionals at Anne Arundel Medical Center. Dr. Hatcher took the initiative to consult with Dr. Hanna, my Pain Management Doctor in Florida, to explore the most effective means of supporting my healthcare needs. It is evident that he invested time and effort into comprehending the complexities of this debilitating disease.

RSD/CRPS stands as the most excruciating disease documented in medical history.

RSD/CRPS, can be elucidated by likening the state of the nerves to that of being raw and lacking insulation, rendering them vulnerable to their surroundings. Analogous to an electrical line devoid of insulation, these nerves can be considered live wires, wherein any form of stimulation results in excessive sensitivity and subsequent severe inflammation. Consequently, even minor triggers such as abrupt temperature changes or major events like surgical interventions aimed at malignancy removal can prompt nerve inflammation. Once inflamed, the nerves undergo a repetitive oscillation beneath the skin, resembling the motion of an active electrical wire that has been toppled by a storm. Consequently, as the nerves approach the surface of the skin or other organs, the intense heat emitted by the nerves scalds anything in its path.

Dr. Hatcher was well aware that the cancer surgery would incite significant upheaval within my body, especially considering that the lymph nodes requiring removal were situated in close proximity to the already compromised nerves resulting from prior spinal surgeries.

Your New Day Dawning

Maryland, like several other states, adheres to an exceedingly cautious approach regarding the administration of pain medication during and after surgical procedures, attributing it to the ongoing opioid crisis.

If the surgical removal of the cancer were to induce a flare, an intense and protracted episode of excruciating pain that could endure for varying durations, the medical practitioners in Maryland would be unable to administer a sufficient quantity of pain medication to effectively alleviate the anticipated level of distress. To address this concern, the prudent course of action would involve administering a judicious dosage of ketamine at the appropriate juncture, thereby assuaging the nervous system and preemptively mitigating the occurrence of the flare.

Despite his unfamiliarity with this particular protocol, Dr. Hatcher exhibited exceptional dedication by proactively researching and acquiring comprehensive knowledge regarding RSD/CRPS and ketamine protocols, with the primary objective of ensuring the provision of optimal healthcare for myself and any other patient under his anesthesiology care.

It is worth noting that Dr. Hatcher's commitment to going above and beyond was entirely voluntary and extended beyond the scope of his responsibilities towards me or any other individual seeking his professional expertise.

Lady Kimberly Motes Doty

During my stay in the recovery room, I engaged in a conversation with the recovery nurse, who I recall goes by the name of Julie. She attested to Dr Hatcher's unwavering commitment towards his patients, meticulously conducting comprehensive research to ascertain their individual needs and ensuring that he possessed the necessary proficiency to offer optimal assistance. Truly, I must express my utmost satisfaction with the remarkable team of healthcare professionals at Anne Arundel Medical Center, as I could not have asked for a more dedicated and proficient group of individuals. It is worth noting that Julie, in addition to her exceptional competence, exhibited an exceptional level of kindness and compassion throughout my recovery process.

Dr. Hatcher, I am immensely grateful to you for the exceptional level of care, compassion, and research you dedicated to my case during one of the most vulnerable periods of my life. Since the successful removal of my cancer, I am pleased to inform you that I did not experienced a single RSD/CRPS flare for over a year.

Considering the profound impact that cancer and its subsequent changes had on both my physical and mental well-being, I cannot stress enough how crucial it was for me to avoid any additional burden such as an RSD/CRPS flare. Your expertise and diligence in ensuring my well-being beyond just the removal of the cancer were truly invaluable.

Your New Day Dawning

Dr. Thomas Prebish, DO

Medical Director of Wound Care Center

Sometimes, the repercussions of cancer treatment necessitate additional surgical interventions. I was introduced to the expertise of Dr. Prebish and his proficient team when I required such supplementary procedures, specifically related to surgical repair and wound management.

One of these surgeries aimed to rectify an unhealed aperture near my belly button following a prior laparoscopic surgery. Whether it had been overlooked or perhaps inadequately sealed, the resulting aperture was significant enough for me to insert a finger into it.

Lady Kimberly Motes Doty

Astonishingly, the presence of this petite hole in proximity to my belly button caused persistent discomfort, as if something was perpetually snagging and pinching me. Dr. Prebish, assisted by his capable associate Jill, skillfully addressed this issue by meticulously repairing the aperture. Unexpectedly, the complexity of the situation surpassed both their expectations and mine, necessitating a three-inch incision below my belly button to secure the "stem" of the belly button alongside the aforementioned aperture. Another occasion called for their expertise in providing meticulous wound care.

Once an individual is diagnosed with cancer, their vulnerability to other types of cancer increases. In my personal case, I had been monitoring a specific area on my breast for a period exceeding fifteen years. Due to my history with Cancer, the medical professionals believed it was in my best interest, from both a health and safety standpoint, to undergo a complete bilateral mastectomy. Prior to the mastectomy, I was engaging in vigorous physical activity, walking approximately 8-12 miles daily along the beach.

It is uncertain whether I did not allow sufficient time for adequate healing or if I resumed walking too soon after the surgery, as the implants became severely infected. Within a few days, my condition deteriorated significantly, leading to intense discomfort. Seeking medical assistance, I promptly consulted my primary care physician, who immediately referred me back to Dr. Prebish.

Dr. Prebish, being both a highly skilled surgeon and the medical director specialized in wound care, brought me right into his office to see him and his staff.

Your New Day Dawning

The infection had escalated to a distressing extent beneath one of my breasts, with the affected area looking to me like it was displaying visible ribs due to the rapid and severe infection. Even on the opposite breast, the infection had already reached a critical stage. Thanks to the swift intervention of Dr. Prebish's office, I was afforded immediate medical attention.

I experienced a profound fear of losing my breasts due to the severity of the infection. It is astonishing how swiftly an infection can disseminate throughout the body following a cancer diagnosis. With the immune system significantly compromised, the ability to combat the infection is greatly diminished. As a woman, undergoing a hysterectomy already feels like relinquishing a vital aspect of femininity. Consequently, the additional loss of my breasts, necessitating replacement, left me with a palpable sense of losing touch with my essence as a woman. The prospect of losing my breasts entirely due to the infection was devastating. It felt as though my womanhood was vanishing altogether. Whether or not they perceived my constant emotional vulnerability, the gentle, efficient, and compassionate care provided by the entire staff had a profoundly soothing effect on me. I will forever remain grateful for their kindness.

From moment I experienced discomfort and became aware of a problem, it took no more than three to four days, at most a week, to reach my Primary Care Doctor, Dr. Prebish. Unfortunately, by that time, the infection had already worsened significantly.

Lady Kimberly Motes Doty

Over a span of approximately six weeks, I visited Dr. Prebish and his assistant, Jill, once a week for wound care. I must commend Dr. Prebish and his entire team for their exceptional levels of compassion, care, and respect.

It was already embarrassing for me to expose my abdomen, with its open wound when I had to have my belly button repaired, but the thought of returning to them so soon and exposing my entire breasts could have been utterly humiliating. However, they treated me with utmost respect, ensuring I was appropriately covered at all times. At no point did I feel like an object on display. Many of us women understand that some doctors and nurses tend to overlook our modesty, making it all the more important when professionals take the time to ensure our comfort and privacy.

Dr. Prebish's assistant, Jill, diligently coordinated regular in-home wound care services on alternate days throughout the required period. This prudent arrangement was implemented amidst the peak of the pandemic, alleviating the need for me to visit the clinic, which would have potentially heightened my vulnerability to infections.

Dr. Prebish, I would like to express my immense gratitude to you and your esteemed staff for the compassionate, attentive, and professional care I have received during my surgeries and wound treatment. Your consistent dedication as a healthcare provider has been an incredible blessing to me. Without your exceptional care, I would not have been able to fulfill my dream of bringing these books to fruition. It is unimaginable how severe the infection could have become or potentially spread throughout my body if you and your team had not responded promptly and with such professionalism.

Your New Day Dawning

The Key to the Success of this Author

The key to the success of this author, who has achieved a number one selling new release book and numerous other highly acclaimed publications, despite battling and recovering from two separate cancer diagnoses and enduring a lifelong struggle with RSD/CRPS, lies not only in divine intervention but also in the compassionate care provided by the doctors who have played an integral role in transforming the author's literary aspirations into reality. Without the assistance of these virtuous individuals, the author's accomplishments would have remained unattainable.

It is an established truth that during times of adversity, God always guides the right person to provide aid and solace. For this author, that divine intervention comes in the form of these doctors who have offered the much-needed care that I desperately sought. Their benevolent demeanor and unparalleled medical expertise have profoundly impacted both my life and my heart in numerous ways. The influence of their compassionate attention is immeasurable, and it has forever altered my being.

This author expresses profound gratitude towards God for the fortuitous encounter with these empathetic doctors. Their divine approach to patient care is greatly appreciated. This author firmly believes that these doctors consistently demonstrate an unparalleled level of compassion towards all patients, solidifying their status as genuine healers.

The impact of these doctors on my life is immeasurable. They have provided the necessary support and fortitude to pursue my dreams, for which I remain eternally grateful.

My message is simple yet powerful:

In order to achieve success, one requires individuals who genuinely care.

For this author, these remarkable doctors have served as unwavering sources of strength throughout my journey.

~Lady Kimberly

Your New Day Dawning

Contents

Dedication 4

Acknowledgment 7

   To My Family 7

   To My Doctors 8

      Dr. Asraf Hanna, MD..8

      Dr Claudia Hays, MD..11

      Dr. Monica Jones, MD 18

      Dr Charles Hatcher, MD.......................................22

      Dr. Thomas Prebish, DO 26

      The Key to the Success of this Author 30

Introduction..39

A New Day Is Dawning 1

   Endless Ever Changing Skylines 2

   Regeneration - Your New Day Dawning 3

   Shoreline Early Mornings....................................18

   An Ever Changing Canvas of Colors 19

   A Surreal Time of Day 20

   If You Blink, You Miss The Colors Changing 21

Early Morning Walks Along The Gulf Coast 23

I Feel Closest To God 24

I Hear His Voice Among The Chaos...25

Why Jesus Has His Routine Prayer Times 26

Quiet Early Mornings 27

Prayer And Meditation Times..28

Prayer 29

Meditation...33

Nothing Will Ever Compare To The Peace And Joy 42

The Ever Changing Colors 43

They Change With Every Step You Take 44

Sunrises 45

Your New Day Dawning..45

The Effervescent Mornings 47

Permeates My Soul Bringing Me Closer to Our Creator...........48

My Soul Waits For The Lord 49

His Coming Is as Brilliant as The Sunrise................................51

The Magical Melody of Colors 54

Even Before The Sunrise I Pray For Your Help 55

Great Is His Faithfulness...57

    Great Is His Faithfulness 57

    Each Day Is A New Inspiration 59

    An Endless Flow Of Gods Glory Before Us 60

    As A Morning Blessing To Start Each Day 61

    The Rising Sun Will Come From Heaven 62

    He Guides Our Feet Into The Path Of Peace 64

He Is Like The Brightness After Rain................................65

    He Is Like the Light of Morning Sunrise 65

From The Rising of The Sun...67

    From The Rising Sum..67

    East To West, His Name Is Praised..69

    The Majesty Of His Creation Is Revered 70

    The Lord God Is Brighter Than The Brilliance Of A Sunrise ...71

    At Each And Every Sunrise, You Will Hear My Voice...............73

    Every morning I lay out the pieces of my life on the altar 75

Sand Sculptures..76

The Sculptor 76

Alligator 78

Octopus 79

Octopus 2 80

Crab 81

Squid 82

Turtle 83

Hippopotamus 84

Gothic Castle 85

Scottish Castle 86

Castle Compound 87

Snail 88

Pink Flamingo 89

Feather Castle 90

Pumpkin 91

Starfish / Sea Star 92

    Natural Healing - Renewal and Healing 92

    Starfish Is Really a Sea Star 92

Symbolic Meaning of Sea Stars In Christian Culture 96

Pink Sea Star 100

Lone Sea Star 101

Bubbly Sea Star 102

Shelly Sea Stars 103

Wind Blown Sea Star 104

Curvy Sea Star 105

Upside Down Sea Star 106

Regenerating Sea Star 107

Pair Of Sea Stars 108

Lady Kimberly Published Books 109

A Godly Way of Life 109

If The Alphabet Grew Out Of The Sea 110

 Children's Activity Book 110

Si El Alfabeto Creció Fuera De Mar 111

Si l'Alphabet A Grandi Hors De La Mer 112

Pregnancy, Nausea and Vomiting 113

 A Pregnancy Nausea and Vomiting Basics Handbook 113

Inspirationals, Quotes and Sayings 114

The Belly Dance Pilates Walking Program 115
    The Easy Way To Benefit From Pilates and Belly Dance Walking 115

Life As Cake 116
    Learning To Manage Life So Life Doesn't Manage You 116

The Sea And The Princess 117
    The Sea Whispers To Me 117

A Children's Guide To A Godly Life 118
    Learning To Live Your Life The Way Jesus Did 118

About the Author 119
    Lady Kimberly Motes Doty 119

Your New Day Dawning

Page Blank Intentionally

Lady Kimberly Motes Doty

Introduction

I am a big prayer.

I pray about everything.

I am one of those people who pray so much I wondered if God was tired of hearing from me at one point in my life.

Have you ever gone through one of those times in your life? To some extent, I think we all have. Even Jesus called out to God asking "why have you forsaken me" when He was on the cross.

My God, my God, why have you forsaken me? Why are you so far from saving me, so far from my cries of anguish? My God, I cry out by day, but you do not answer, by night, but I find no rest. Psalm 22:1-2

Have you ever felt that tired, that utterly exhausted, like Jesus did when He cried out, saying, "why are you so far from saving me, so far from my cries of anguish? My God, I cry out by day, but you don't answer, by night, but I find no rest…"

My God, my God, why have you forsaken me? Why are you so far from saving me, so far from my cries of anguish? My God, I cry out by day, but you do not answer, by night, but I find no rest. Psalm 22:1-2

Lady Kimberly Motes Doty

I found myself there a few times in the worst of the cancer recoveries and I still find myself here at times from the nerve condition I have. I have had two different types of cancer and I have what has been reported to be the most painful disease known to exist. It is a nerve disease that causes excruciating pain that given this crack down on pain medications, nothing cuts through the pain and it will get so awful, I will pass out from the sheer extent of the pain. I know nothing can possibly compare to the horrendous pain Jesus must have felt when he was on the cross crying out to God.

About three in the afternoon Jesus cried out in a loud voice, "Eli, Eli, lemasabachthani?" which means "My God, my God, why have you forsaken me?"). Matthew 27:46

And at three in the afternoon Jesus cried in a loud voice, "Elio, Elio, lema sabachthani?" (which means "My God, my God, why have you forsaken me?"). Mark 15:34

Even Jesus's human side cried out to God when He felt like God was no longer hearing Him. So as a human, we all wonder if God still hears us sometimes.

I pray all the time, not because I think I need God's permission to do anything in my life. I know He already knows everything that will ever happen and everything that could ever happened.

About three in the afternoon Jesus cried out in a loud voice, "Eli, Eli, lemasabachthani?" which means "My God, my God, why have you forsaken me?").
Matthew 27:46, Mark 15:34

Lady Kimberly Motes Doty

I am a big prayer.

I pray all the time.

I pray all the time to seek His guidance and blessing for everything I do. I know God created a life plan for my life long before I was ever created, long before mankind ever existed and long before the earth even existed. I pray to make sure everything I do is inline with God's plan for my life.

It seems so deceptively simple doesn't it?

However, sometimes what I want doesn't always align with God's plan for my life or God's timing for my life. Praying is my way of helping align the two.

My favorite time of day to begin my prayers is just before the sunrise. I have been blessed with living close enough to the beach to be able to walk on the beach to pray most days. This book is a compilation of some of my favorite photos from my early morning walks along the Gulf of Mexico beaches here in the Tampa area and perhaps some even from my trips to the Carolina beaches.

Just as Jesus loved to begin his days with an early morning prayer along the Sea of Galilee with a quiet communion with God, I find my early morning walks give me the most inspiration and closest prayer time with God.

A prayer is a quiet conversation with God. A prayer is a focused meditation to help align God's plan for your life with your will or your wants for your life. It is your personal time with God. If there ever was a time to totally fall in love with God with all your heart, soul and mind, this is the time to get to know Him and make that happen.

Many times I've heard people say, I can't really pray but I can meditate.

If you can meditate, you can pray.

Meditation requires a quiet mind. Prayer requires a quiet mind. Prayer allows you to take your plans, hopes, dreams, fears, aspirations, doubts, and any other thoughts you have about anything in your life and talk to the one who created you about these things to help create a more quieted, calmed, focused, organized mind. Often, during my prayer time, I come away with exactly what I have been looking for and needing to solve or answer my needs during my prayer time. Prayer time is where God helps us find the solutions we are needing to the questions and issues in our lives.

Furthermore, as the Bible tells us God created a life plan, "plans to prosper, not harm, give hope and a future" for each of us long before we were ever created, long before the heavens and the earth were ever created. I believe along with the life plan God created for each of us, He instilled in us, the hopes, desires and needs to fulfill this life plan He created for us. Along with the hopes, desires, and needs He instilled in each of us, He gave us the ability to achieve the life plan He had created for us.

God did not just create an empty promise he gave us everything we need to achieve these plans.

He gave us everything we need to fulfill this promise He was telling us about in Jeremiah 29:11. All we have to do is love Him, with all of our heart, soul and mind as our Creator and only God, Matthew 22:37-40 tells us.

Jeremiah 29:11. "For I know the plans I have for you," declares the LORD, "plans to prosper you and not to harm you, plans to give you hope and a future."

"For I know the plans I have for you," declares the LORD, "plans to prosper you and not to harm you, plans to give you hope and a future." Jeremiah 29:11

Lady Kimberly Motes Doty

"And he said to him, "You shall love the Lord your God with all your heart and with all your soul and with all your mind. This is the great and first commandment. And the second is like it: You shall love your neighbor as yourself. On these two commandments depend all the Law and Prophets." Matthew 22:37-40

"And he said to him, "You shall love the Lord your God with all your heart and with all your soul and with all your mind. This is the great and first commandment. And the second is like it: You shall love your neighbor as yourself. On these two commandments depend all the Law and Prophets."
Matthew 22:37-40

Lady Kimberly Motes Doty

It is my sincere prayer you find inspiration in this book, Your New Day Dawning.

I pray you fall in love with God with all your heart and with all your soul and will all your mind through His beautiful, amazing inspirational beaches, beach life and sunrises that you find in these photographs.

I pray the verses that correspond to these amazing photos touch you and inspire you to know God and seek Him to be your personal savior and best friend.
I pray you come to know God as I have come to know him.

I pray you crave time with Him and crave to know more about his word and more about the life of Jesus so that you can become more like Jesus to allow you to prepared for a life with Him in heaven as a Child of Light, so full of love, God, Jesus and the Holy Spirit that His light shines out of you like a beacon unto the world so everyone sees your light and knows you are one of God's children by this amazing light and the wondrous love you show everyone you come into contact with.

I pray these in Jesus Christ holy name,

~ Lady Kimberly Motes Doty

A New Day Is Dawning

Lady Kimberly Motes Doty

Endless Ever Changing Skylines

Your New Day Dawning

Regeneration - Your New Day Dawning

A regeneration is a new creation. Allow Jesus to create a new creation in you whenever you are ready to begin again as His, to be the person He created you to be, the truly genuine best version of yourself you can be. As 2 Corinthians 5:17 tells us "If anyone is in Christ, he is a new creation; the old is gone, the new has come!"

"If anyone is in Christ, he is a new creation; the old has gone, the new has come!" 2 Corinthians 5:17

This is one of the examples in the Bible that is so important it has an explanation point at the end. I always love those because its a signal to me to pay extra attention to them.

Have you ever felt like it was time in your life to regenerate yourself? A time when you wanted to remake yourself, to recreate yourself, to start over?

Sometimes it's a life event that feels like a natural time to start something new and begin again like a graduation, the birth of baby, starting a new job, getting married, or something wonderful along these lines, all of which again, feel like a natural time to start something new in your life.

> "If anyone is in Christ, he is a new creation; the old has gone, the new has come!"
>
> 2 Corinthians 5:17

Your New Day Dawning

Other times, it is an entirely different life event like a divorce, a death, a terrible accident, some terrible disease, or some devastating tragedy that still falls into a life event because it marks your life forever; but, it doesn't feel natural nor does it feel wonderful.

Sometimes even out of the devastating something wonderful can still emerge.

I know you are definitely thinking, death, divorce, disease, or some other devastation…

How can something wonderful possibly emerge you crazy woman!

I can say this because of God's plan for our lives. I can say this because of God's promise to us when He created this plan for our lives.

God created the plan for your life long before you were ever born, long before He created the heavens and the earth. God's plans for us is to "prosper us, not harm us, to give us hope and a future" as we are promised in Jeremiah 29:11.

"For I know the plans I have for you," declares the Lord, "plans to prosper you and not to harm you, plans to give you hope and a future." Jeremiah 29:11

"For I know the plans I have for you," declares the Lord, "plans to prosper you and not to harm you, plans to give you hope and a future." Jeremiah 29:11

Your New Day Dawning

God will never lie to us, betray us, or forsake us, he promises us this in Numbers 23:19, Titus 1:2, Hebrews 6:18 and Deuteronomy 3:18.

God is not a man, that he should lie; neither the son of man, that he should repent: hath he said, and shall he not do it? or hath he spoken, and shall he not make it good? Numbers 23:19 KJV

In hope of eternal life, which God, that cannot lie, promised before the world began; Titus 1:2

That by two immutable things, in which it was impossible for God to lie, we might have a strong consolation, who have fled for refuge to lay hold upon the hope set before us: Hebrews 6:18

It is the Lord who goes before you. He will be with you; he will not leave you or forsake you. Do not fear or be dismayed. Deuteronomy 31:8

God is not a man, that he should lie; neither the son of man, that he should repent: hath he said, and shall he not do it? or hath he spoken, and shall he not make it good? Numbers 23:19 KJV

In hope of eternal life, which God, that cannot lie, promised before the world began; Titus 1:2

That by two immutable things, in which it was impossible for God to lie, we might have a strong consolation, who have fled for refuge to lay hold upon the hope set before us: Hebrews 6:18

He will never allow anything to come between His love for us and us as he promised us this in.

Romans 8:35-39

Our Creator will never allow anything to come between His love for us and us as he promised us this in Romans 8:35-39

Who shall separate us from the love of Christ? shall tribulation, or distress, or persecution, or famine, or nakedness, or peril, or sword? As it is written, For thy sake we are killed all the day long; we are accounted as sheep for the slaughter. Nay, in all these things we are more than conquerors through him that loved us. For I am persuaded, that neither death, nor life, nor angels, nor principalities, nor powers, nor things present, nor things to come, Nor height, nor depth, nor any other creature, shall be able to separate us from the love of God, which is in Christ Jesus our Lord. Romans 8:35–39 KJV

Isn't this an awesome thing to know? There is nothing that can ever be ever be done or created or undone that will ever separate us from God or change the way God loves us. God's love is so faithful, strong, consistent, powerful, all encompassing and enduring that He will never do anything to change it and He will never allow anyone or anything to ever change it.

Who shall separate us from the love of Christ? shall tribulation, or distress, or persecution, or famine, or nakedness, or peril, or sword? As it is written, For thy sake we are killed all the day long; we are accounted as sheep for the slaughter. Nay, in all these things we are more than conquerors through him that loved us.

For I am persuaded, that neither death, nor life, nor angels, nor principalities, nor powers, nor things present, nor things to come, Nor height, nor depth, nor any other creature, shall be able to separate us from the love of God, which is in Christ Jesus our Lord. Romans 8:35-39 KJV

Lady Kimberly Motes Doty

We may not see or understand the full big picture of what is going on in the world. We may only see and feel the devastation of our our one little piece of it. But God, our LORD, created everything and understands everything and how He created it to all fits together for His Devine plan. Isaiah 55:9 tells us this. Proverbs 3:5-6 tells us to trust in the Lord and not our own understanding; acknowledge Him and he will direct our paths.

To me, this is God's way of tell us to be faithful in our prayers and our belief in Him, in His divine plan for us and He will regenerate us and make us a new creation out of the devastation, making something wonderful, getting us back to the promise of Jeremiah 29:11 to "prosper us, not harm us, to give us hope and a future".

"For my thoughts are not your thoughts, neither are your ways my ways, declares the LORD. For as the heavens are higher than the earth, so are my ways higher than your ways and my thoughts than your thoughts." Isaiah 55:9

Trust in the Lord with all thine heart; and lean not unto thine own understanding. In all thy ways acknowledge him, and he shall direct thy paths. Proverbs 3:5-6

I love this about God, our Creator.

His faithful promises are as relevant today as they have always been.

"For my thoughts are not your thoughts, neither are your ways my ways, declares the LORD. For as the heavens are higher than the earth, so are my ways higher than your ways and my thoughts than your thoughts." Isaiah 55:9

Trust in the Lord with all thine heart; and lean not unto thine own understanding. In all thy ways acknowledge him, and he shall direct thy paths. Proverbs 3:5-6

Your New Day Dawning

His promise that He has a plan for us, to prosper us, not harm us, to give us hope and a future" always gives me hope on some of my darkest days. Just knowing our creator created me with a plan for my life gives me hope.

I have some really dark days sometimes. I have chronic nerve pain disease and I've had two different types of cancer. Some days are just more difficult than others, right?

We all have things we deal with….

Knowing our creator regenerates us is a precious and a saving grace, isn't it?

Knowing that nothing is beyond what He can recreate and regenerate gives me hope for your new day dawning.

All I have to do is believe and accept Him, love and honor Him.

Shoreline Early Mornings

Nothing can be more beautiful than walking along the shoreline in the early mornings.

Your New Day Dawning

An Ever Changing Canvas of Colors

The sky is an ever changing canvas of colors and the waves are ever changing colors of lavender, purple, turquoise, blue and green.

Lady Kimberly Motes Doty

A Surreal Time of Day

It is almost surreal at this time of day.

Your New Day Dawning

If You Blink, You Miss The Colors Changing

Lady Kimberly Motes Doty

It's one of those moments in your life where literally, if you blink, you miss the colors changing before your eyes.

Your New Day Dawning

Early Morning Walks Along The Gulf Coast

It is during these early morning walks along the Gulf Coast

I Feel Closest To God

Especially in the early mornings, where it's just me and my prayers, my private conversations with our creator, that I feel the closest to God

Your New Day Dawning

I Hear His Voice Among The Chaos

It's in these early morning prayer times that I His voice among the chaos of the early mornings.

Why Jesus Has His Routine Prayer Times

Have you ever thought about why Jesus had his routine prayer times or why they happen to coincide with the changing of the colors in the sky?

Your New Day Dawning

Quiet Early Mornings

It's in the quiet early mornings and the late afternoons that I imaging Jesus walking his daily walk around the Sea of Galilee, softly talking with His disciples.

Prayer And Meditation Times

I see myself doing the same things as I have my prayer and meditation times out here.

Your New Day Dawning

Prayer

Jesus taught us prayer is a quiet conversation with our creator, with God as He explains to us in Matthew 6:5-8. When you pray, you quiet your mind and have a conversation with God, one on one, like you were talking to your best friend, your Mom or Dad.

Have you ever tried to have a conversation with your best friend or your Mom or Dad in a crowded place with lots of chaos going on around you? It isn't very easy to hear or focus on what is being said or hearing what is being said, is it?

The same is true with trying to have prayer time in a crowded chaotic place, Your mind has a much harder time focusing on what is on your mind, or on your heart, let alone what you wanted to talk to God, your best friend or Mom or Dad about with so much going on around you. This is why Jesus teaches us to find a quiet place to have our prayer time.

And when thou prayest, thou shalt not be as the hypocrites are: for they love to pray standing in the synagogues and in the corners of the streets, that they may be seen of men. Verily I say unto you, They have their reward. But thou, when thou prayest, enter into thy closet, and when thou hast shut thy door, pray to thy Father which is in secret; and thy Father which seeth in secret shall reward thee openly. But when ye pray, use not vain repetitions, as the heathen do: for they think that they shall be heard for their much speaking. Be not ye therefore like unto them: for your Father knoweth what things ye have need of, before ye ask him. Matthew 6:5-8 KJV

And when thou prayest, thou shalt not be as the hypocrites are: for they love to pray standing in the synagogues and in the corners of the streets, that they may be seen of men. Verily I say unto you, They have their reward. But thou, when thou prayest, enter into thy closet, and when thou hast shut thy door, pray to thy Father which is in secret; and thy Father which seeth in secret shall reward thee openly. But when ye pray, use not vain repetitions, as the heathen do: for they think that they shall be heard for their much speaking. Be not ye therefore like unto them: for your Father knoweth what things ye have need of, before ye ask him. Matthew 6:5-8 KJV

Jesus also teaches us our Creator already knows what we need, and that He only needs us to talk to Him and ask Him anyway. God wants a close relationship with us.

Just as we want close relationships with the people we love, God wants us to create and cultivate a close relationship with Him. The Bible tells us God will rejoice over us with gladness, quiet us with his love, exult over us with loud singing.

The Lord your God is in your midst, a mighty one who will save; he will rejoice over you with gladness; he will quiet you by his love; he will exult over you with loud singing. Zephaniah 3:17 ESV

Can you imagine this?

Our creator loving us, loving you so much that he rejoices over *you* with gladness! He quiets you with His love! God rejoices over you with loud singing!

God really wants this close relationship with us this much! He wants us to want to know Him.

The Lord your God is in your midst, a mighty one who will save; he will rejoice over you with gladness; he will quiet you by his love; he will exult over you with loud singing. Zephaniah 3:17 ESV

Meditation

Meditation in its simplest form is focusing of the mind.

Meditating is also biblical.

The primary difference between biblical meditation and eastern meditation from this point on is biblical meditation focuses on drawing closer to God, our Creator and the scriptures while eastern meditation focuses on withdrawing from everything around you and focusing on losing yourself more into the universal aspects of things.

How blessed is the man
who does not walk in the counsel of the wicked,
Nor stand in the path of sinners,
Nor sit in the seat of scoffers!
But his delight is in the law of the Lord,
And in His law he meditates day and night.
He will be like a tree firmly planted by streams of water,
Which yields its fruit in its season
And its leaf does not wither;
And in whatever he does, he prospers. Psalm 1:1-3

How blessed is the man
who does not walk in the counsel of the wicked,
Nor stand in the path of sinners,
Nor sit in the seat of scoffers!
But his delight is in the law of the Lord,
And in His law he meditates day and night.
He will be like a tree firmly planted by streams of water,
Which yields its fruit in its season
And its leaf does not wither;
And in whatever he does, he prospers.
Psalm 1:1-3

Your New Day Dawning

Meditating on our Creator and on the scriptures helps us understand our Creator better and to fall in love with all of our heart, soul and mind as we have been commanded to do by Jesus in Matthew 22:37.

Jesus said unto him, Thou shalt love the Lord thy God with all thy heart, and with all thy soul, and with all thy mind.
Matthew 22:37 KJV

Have you ever fallen in love with another person, a human?

It's the same kind of feeling to fall in love with God, our creator only better. The unconditional love our Creator, God returns back is felt in the heart, soul and mind in much the same way as it is when we fall in love with another person however it is multiplied by a factor of about a million I would say!

It touches everything inside of you and transforms you in way nothing else ever could.

Jesus said unto him,
Thou shalt love the Lord thy God with all thy heart, and with all thy soul, and with all thy mind.
Matthew 22:37 KJV

The Bible talks about being a "new creature" when you are "in Christ" this is exactly what you are in 2 Corinthians 5:17. You are a new creation and the old things have truly passed away.

Therefore if anyone is in Christ, he is a new creature; the old things passed away; behold, new things have come.
2 Corinthians 5:17

Falling in love with our Creator is one of the sweetest blessings of life, of existence. Although we are commanded to fall in love with our heart, soul and mind, falling in love isn't something that happens on command, is it?

We can't even make ourselves fall in love with the "right" one when the right one is a human, can we? However, we have all known that person that initially we weren't attracted to but when we got to know them, something about the way they spoke, or something they were passionate about or just something about them, we found really really attractive.

What we didn't realize is that we were "meditating" on this person. We were thinking about them, we were taking the time to really concentrate on what they were saying or doing, which is what meditation is. This is what allowed us to "fall in love" with them. This is how meditation works with falling in love with our creator with our entire heart, all our soul, and all our mind. Without this time spent really getting to know the scriptures and spending this intimate time with our creator, I don't know that falling in love this deeply, this completely, this fully would happen.

Therefore if anyone is in Christ, he is a new creature; the old things passed away; behold, new things have come.
2 Corinthians 5:17

Lady Kimberly Motes Doty

I know for me, personally, this is when it happened. It was during my morning prayer and meditation time spent intimately with our creator. It was when I was talking, which is to say, praying heart to heart, my soul wide open, in earnest conversation to my best friend, my savior, my God, about everything in my heart, my soul and on. my mind about what I was reading in the Bible, what I was learning, what I understood, what I didn't, what was happening in my life, what was happening in the world… I talked to God about everything just like I was talking to my very best friend in the world because to me, He is my best friend. He will never betray my heart. He will never tell anyone my deepest secrets. He will always be as deeply in love with me as I am with Him except He always loves me more than I could ever love Him so He is always the one more in love. No matter how much I love Him, He will always love me more. No matter what I do, he will always forgive me when I ask Him to forgive me earnestly. He knows my heart better than anyone else. He knows me and loves me on my best days. Even more importantly He knows me and he loves me even more on my worst days. The more time I spend, in prayer and meditation with Him, with God, our creator, the more deeply I fall in love with Him. It is the sweetest most fulfilling relationship of my entire life.

The sweet, amazing contentment I get from this prayer and meditation time exceeds anything I have ever experienced from anything else in my life. When read, Psalm 104:34 about hoping my meditation is pleasing to him and how I rejoice in the Lord! My heart expands and the love for Him and tears overflow down my cheeks. This is real love. This is soul contentment. My heart is at ease.

"May my meditation be pleasing to him, as I rejoice in the Lord." Psalm 104:34

Lady Kimberly Motes Doty

Nothing Will Ever Compare To The Peace And Joy

Nothing will ever compare to the peace and joy I find here.

Your New Day Dawning

The Ever Changing Colors

The ever changing colors are a breathtaking wonder to behold.

They Change With Every Step You Take

It's almost as if they change with every step you take

Sunrises

Your New Day Dawning

"Light is sweet; how pleasant to see a new day dawning." Ecclesiastes 11:7 NLT

Your New Day Dawning

The Effervescent Mornings

Lady Kimberly Motes Doty

Permeates My Soul Bringing Me Closer to Our Creator

Your New Day Dawning

My Soul Waits For The Lord

"My soul waits for the Lord More than those who watch for the morning– Yes, more than those who watch for the morning." Psalm 130:6 NKJV

His Coming Is as Brilliant as The Sunrise

"His coming is as brilliant as the sunrise. Rays of light flash from his hands, where his awesome power is hidden." Habakkuk 3:4 NLT

Lady Kimberly Motes Doty

"His coming is as brilliant as the sunrise. Rays of light flash from his hands, where his awesome power is hidden."
Habakkuk 3:4 NLT

Lady Kimberly Motes Doty

The Magical Melody of Colors

Your New Day Dawning

Even Before The Sunrise I Pray For Your Help

"Even before sunrise, I pray for your help, and I put my hope in what you have said."
Psalm 119:147 CEV

Great Is His Faithfulness

Great Is His Faithfulness

"Great is his faithfulness; his mercies begin afresh each morning."
Lamentations 3:23 NLT

"Great is his faithfulness; his mercies begin afresh each morning."
Lamentations 3:23 NLT

Your New Day Dawning

Each Day Is A New Inspiration

Lady Kimberly Motes Doty

An Endless Flow Of Gods Glory Before Us

Your New Day Dawning

As A Morning Blessing To Start Each Day

Lady Kimberly Motes Doty

The Rising Sun Will Come From Heaven

"Because of the tender mercy of our God by which the rising sun will come to us from heaven to shine on those living in darkness and in the shadow of death, to guide our feet into the path of peace."
Luke 1:78-79 NIV

Lady Kimberly Motes Duty

He Guides Our Feet Into The Path Of Peace

Your New Day Dawning

He Is Like The Brightness After Rain

He Is Like the Light of Morning Sunrise

He is like the light of morning at sunrise on a cloudless morning, like the brightness after rain that brings grass from the earth."
2 Samuel 23:4 NIV

From The Rising of The Sun

From The Rising Sum

"From the rising of the sun to the going down of it and from east to west, the name of the Lord is to be praised!"
Psalm 113:3 AMPC

"From the rising of the sun to the going down of it and from east to west, the name of the Lord is to be praised!"
Psalm 113:3 AMPC

Your New Day Dawning

East To West, His Name Is Praised

Lady Kimberly Motes Doty

The Majesty Of His Creation Is Revered

Your New Day Dawning

The Lord God Is Brighter Than The Brilliance Of A Sunrise

"For the Lord God is brighter than the brilliance of a sunrise! Wrapping himself around me like a shield, he is so generous with his gifts of grace and glory. Those who walk along his paths with integrity will never lack one thing they need, for he provides it all!"
Psalm 84:11 TPT

Your New Day Dawning

At Each And Every Sunrise, You Will Hear My Voice

"At each and every sunrise you will hear my voice as I prepare my sacrifice of prayer to you. Every morning I lay out the pieces of my life on the altar and wait for your fire to fall upon my heart."
Psalm 5:3 TPT

Your New Day Dawning

Every morning I lay out the pieces of my life on the altar

Sand Sculptures

The Sculptor

Like the sand sculptor on the beach sculpts the sand into the endless creations on the beaches, God can recreate you into the best future version of you. All you have to do is ask.

Originally, the chapter of Ezekiel was a prophecy concerning the desolations of the land of Israel. The chapter talks about the causes, return of the people to Israel, the fruitfulness of it, and of spiritual blessings bestowed upon them in the latter day. The chapter continues with talking about how the enemies of Israel will suffer a vengeance of God's wrath, how the land will become fruitful, the cities will be rebuilt, and the land no more liable to destruction or reproach of the Heathen.

While this was originally a message regarding Israel, it can also be applied to us because if God can do this for an entire nation, He can surely do this for and individual that He loves so much, right? If our Creator can give a "new heart and a new spirit" to a nation, He can give us a new heart and a new spirit too, can't He? Of course He can, He is God, He can do anything, He can do everything. Just as a sculptor takes a mound of sand on the beach and makes a beautiful piece of artwork from it, our Creator, can take your broken and battered heart and spirit and regenerate you into a new creature.

And I will give you a new heart, and a new spirit I will put within you. And I will remove the heart of stone from your flesh and give you a heart of flesh. Ezekiel 36:26 ESV

And I will give you a new heart, and a new spirit I will put within you. And I will remove the heart of stone from your flesh and give you a heart of flesh.
Ezekiel 36:26 ESV

Alligator

Your New Day Dawning

Octopus

Lady Kimberly Motes Doty

Octopus 2

Your New Day Dawning

Crab

Lady Kimberly Motes Doty

Squid

Your New Day Dawning

Turtle

Lady Kimberly Motes Doty

Hippopotamus

Your New Day Dawning

Gothic Castle

Lady Kimberly Motes Doty

Scottish Castle

Your New Day Dawning

Castle Compound

Lady Kimberly Motes Doty

Snail

Your New Day Dawning

Pink Flamingo

Lady Kimberly Motes Doty

Feather Castle

Your New Day Dawning

Pumpkin

Starfish / Sea Star

Natural Healing - Renewal and Healing

In Natural Healing, we use Starfish as a Symbol to represents our bodies ability to renew and heal ourselves.

The Starfish reminds us of the awesome power and secret to healing and reinventing ourself resides within you. Additionally, the starfish spirit animal represents heightened senses and sensory feelings. It encourages us to trust our instincts and listen to our inner voice.

Among sea creatures, we have both the starfish and the Octopus, which can regrow arms and tentacles. This astonishing capacity makes this animal a symbol of regeneration and healing.

Starfish Is Really a Sea Star

A Starfish name is actually a misnomer. Their real name is Sea Star! Isn't that amazing? They do not have gills, scales, or fins like fish do. So because they are not classified as fish, scientists prefer to call starfish "sea stars."

Inside of us, we really do have this capability. God chose to use the rib of Adam to create us as Women because the rib can regenerate itself.

According to the National Library of Medicine "Fractures to major bones often heal slowly or incompletely, especially in older people, and large bone injuries do not repair naturally. By comparison, rib bones show an unusual capacity to regrow and repair themselves even when a large portion is damaged. Previous research suggests that the connective tissue around the ribs helps to support and coordinate bone healing."

Jesus also tells us if we have Faith as much as the size of a mustard seed, we can move mountains.

"For truly I tell you, if you have faith the size of a mustard seed, you will say to this mountain, 'Move from here to there,' and it will move; and nothing will be impossible for you." Matthew 17:20-21

Our thoughts are things. What we believe becomes our reality. What we say to ourselves the most, we make happen in our lives.

With our children, what we say to them most, we make their reality too. If we tell them they are beautiful, intelligent, and loved, this is what they become. If we tell them they are lazy, useless and worthless, sadly, this is also what they become. Thoughts are powerful things, especially to a young mind that is forming and believing everything we tell them.

Remember, as a parent, you are their entire world for so many years of their life. What you tell them IS their reality.

What do you you really want your precious child to believe about themselves? That they are precious, loved and learning? Or they are a clumsy, stupid, nuisance to you?

Every word and reaction from you forms their perception of themselves.

"For truly I tell you, if you have faith the size of a mustard seed, you will say to this mountain, 'Move from here to there,' and it will move; and nothing will be impossible for you."
Matthew 17:20-21

Your New Day Dawning

Be a Sea Star to yourself and your child. Make a conscious choice every day to be kind to yourself and your child. Think before you speak. That's all it takes is one fragile moment of thought before you open your mouth.

You can shape your life and everyone around you by what you say and do with every action, reaction and word you say. Right? Yes, you can. You have the power!

YOU are the only one in charge of YOU and YOUR THOUGHTS and YOUR MOUTH!

YOU CAN choose to build each other up instead of tear each other down.

You really do have the power to do this. Only you! Isn't that amazing? Doesn't it feel good to know you have the power and control to do this?

You can do it! God and Jesus have faith in you! I have faith in you! You are a Sea Star! Regardless of anything in your past, you can decide right here right now to regenerate yourself and be whatever you want to be.

Go forth and be kind to yourself. Be kind to those who depend upon you. Be kind to those who aren't kind to you, chances are they need it the most.

You have the power, You are in control of you. You can do this!

My Sea Star, You can do this! Believe it and do it!

Imagine how good it will feel when you see the changes in those around you.

Imagine how good you will feel when you see the changes in yourself.

Take your power back! You are a Sea Star! Regenerate yourself!

Life the life you really want to live.

Symbolic Meaning of Sea Stars In Christian Culture

The Virgin Mary was given the name Sella Maris, the star of the sea as the defender of the destitute in some Christian literature and early manuscripts. She encouraged troubled people and the disadvantaged have faith in themselves and their abilities.

As the Star of the Sea, the Virgin Mary became a symbol of faith and early Christians believed that if they saw a sea star they would gain favor and protection in the eyes of the Virgin Mary. They looked to Sella Maris, their Star of the Sea for motivation, love, and spiritual fulfillment.

Your New Day Dawning

Christians also believe the sea star is a symbol of love, a symbol of God's wondrous works of creation.

The Sea Star also reminds Christians of the greatest commandment in the Bible, the commandment to love love the Lord your God with all your heart.

Jesus said unto him, Thou shalt love the Lord thy God with all thy heart, and with all thy soul, and with all thy mind.
Matthew 22:37 KJV

We talked earlier about falling in love with the Lord, thy God with all thy heart, and with all thy soul and with all thy mind. How cool is it that the sea star is the symbol for this!

And the sea star is also the symbol for regeneration and becoming a new creation!

So whether your need for regeneration is a natural type life event like graduation and it's a natural time to start something new in your life.

Or if its something different but still a natural life event like the child birth, getting married, starting a new job, or something wonderful along these lines, but still a in the natural life event genre making it a time to start something new in your life.

Jesus said unto him, Thou shalt love the Lord thy God with all thy heart, and with all thy soul, and with all thy mind.
Matthew 22:37 KJV

Your New Day Dawning

Even when it is the entirely different life event like a divorce, a death, a terrible accident, cancer or some other life altering disease, or some devastating tragedy that creates your life event. It marks your life forever.

God is here waiting to make something wonderful out of the devastating or just the life changing. Something wonderful can emerge from whatever the life event happens to be.

This is the beauty of life.

This is the beauty of God's never ending plan for our lives.

This is the beauty of God's never ending love for us.

Pink Sea Star

Your New Day Dawning

Lone Sea Star

Lady Kimberly Motes Doty

Bubbly Sea Star

Your New Day Dawning

Shelly Sea Stars

Lady Kimberly Motes Doty

Wind Blown Sea Star

Your New Day Dawning

Curvy Sea Star

Lady Kimberly Motes Doty

Upside Down Sea Star

Your New Day Dawning

Regenerating Sea Star

Lady Kimberly Motes Doty

Pair Of Sea Stars

Your New Day Dawning

Lady Kimberly Published Books

A Godly Way of Life

Lady Kimberly Motes Doty

If The Alphabet Grew Out Of The Sea

Children's Activity Book

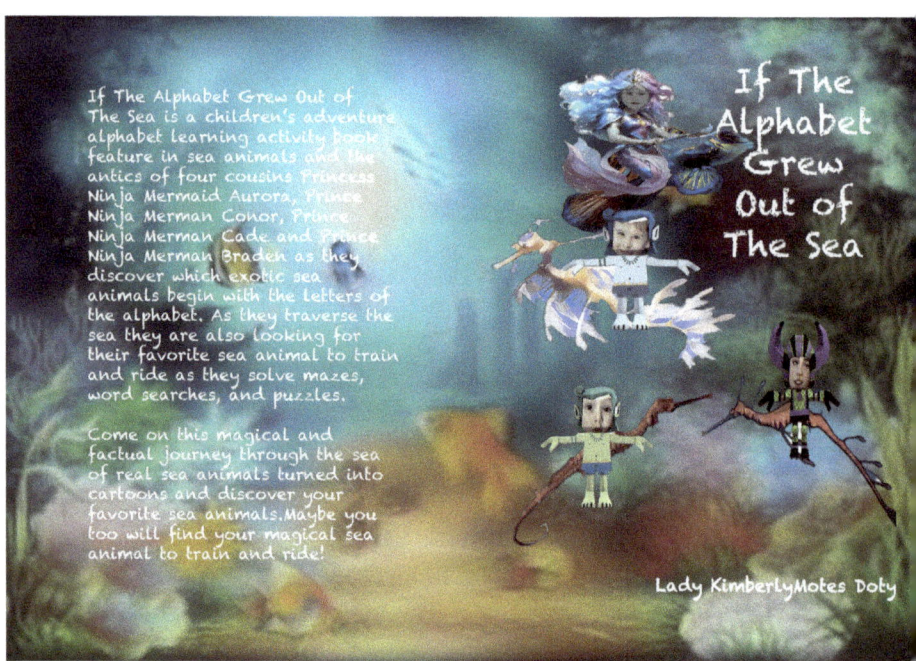

Si El Alfabeto Creció Fuera De Mar

Lady Kimberly Motes Doty

Si l'Alphabet A Grandi Hors De La Mer

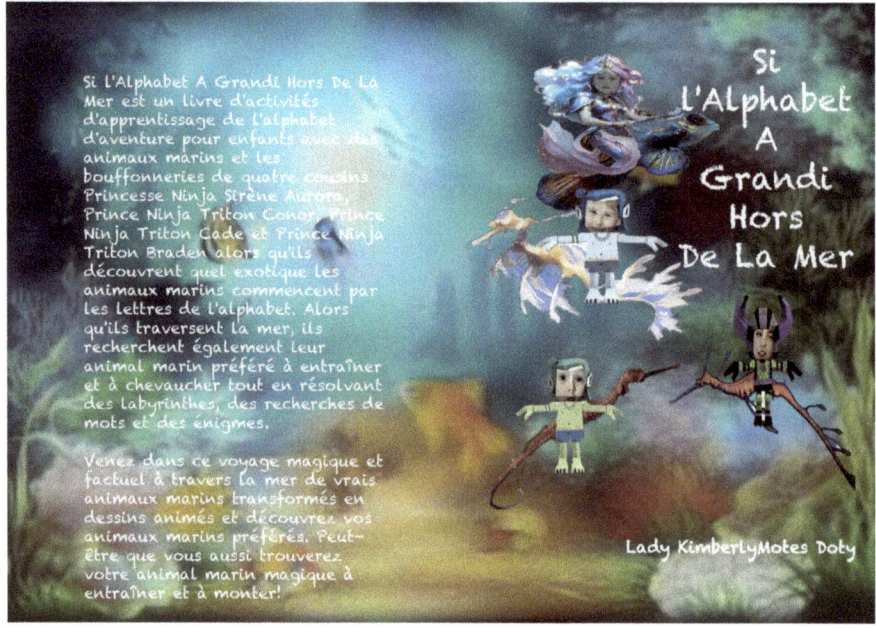

Your New Day Dawning

Pregnancy, Nausea and Vomiting

A Pregnancy Nausea and Vomiting Basics Handbook

Lady Kimberly Motes Doty

Inspirationals, Quotes and Sayings

It Isn't The Life We Start With That Matters. It Is The Life We Make for Ourselves.

Your New Day Dawning

The Belly Dance Pilates Walking Program
The Easy Way To Benefit From Pilates and Belly Dance Walking

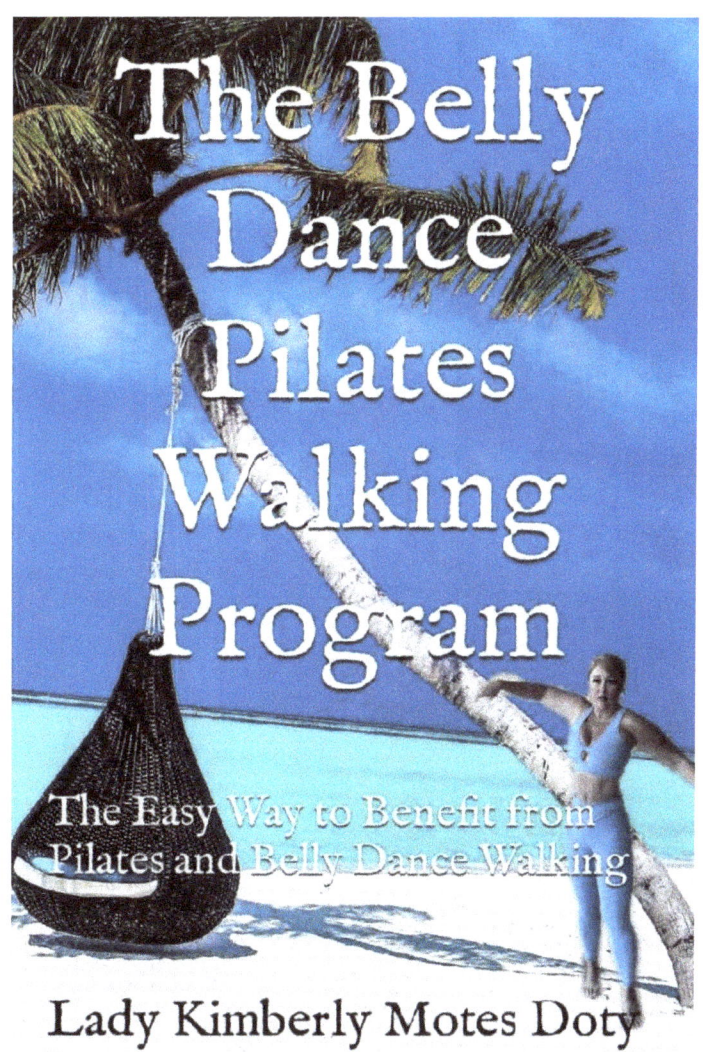

Lady Kimberly Motes Doty

Life As Cake

Learning To Manage Life So Life Doesn't Manage You

Your New Day Dawning

The Sea And The Princess

The Sea Whispers To Me

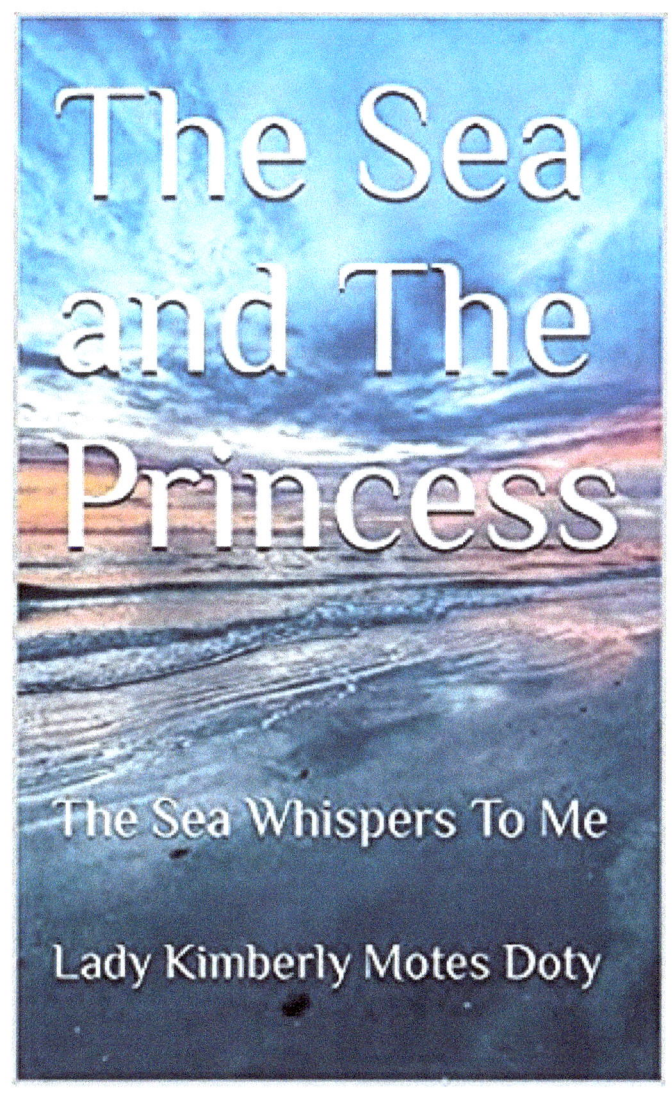

Lady Kimberly Motes Doty

A Children's Guide To A Godly Life
Learning To Live Your Life The Way Jesus Did

About the Author

Lady Kimberly Motes Doty

Lady Kimberly Motes Doty

Lady Kimberly is a Naturopathic Doctor, Certified Natural Health Professional, an Inspirational Speaker, Ordained Minister and an accomplished author. She spends her mornings walking the beaches of the Gulf of Mexico in the Tampa Bay Area and the Beaches of the Carolina's praying and looking for inspiration for her writing and photography.

To follow Lady Kimberly, her Amazon Author page is:

https://www.amazon.com/author/ladykimberly

Your New Day Dawning

Look for more of Lady Kimberly's current and upcoming books:

A Children's Guide to a Godly Way of Life - Just Published
A Godly Way of Life - Published
Your New Day Dawning - #1 New Release
Emma and Luna's Crazy Fat Tail Adventure - Coming Soon
Faith and Fear - Coming Soon
Heaven - Coming Soon
If the Alphabet Grew Out of The Sea - Published & V2 out Soon
Praying Specific For The Life God Intended For You - Coming Soon
Pregnancy, Nausea & Vomiting - Top 10 New Release
Si El Alfabeto Creció Fuera De Mar (Spanish Edition) - Published v2 Soon
Si l'Alphabet A Grandi Hors De La Mer (French Edition) - Published v2 Soon
Spiritual Gifts of the Holy Spirit - Coming Soon
The Bellydance Walking Pilates Program - Top 10 New Release
The Mermaid and The Pillar - Coming Soon
The Princess and The Sea: The Sea Whispers To Me - Top 10 New Release
The Wounds The Won't Heal - Coming Soon
Life As A Cake - Top 10 New Release

www.ingramcontent.com/pod-product-compliance
Lightning Source LLC
Chambersburg PA
CBHW051547010526
44118CB00022B/2614